E.M.E.S.
WAL...
RAD...
RAD...
SHREWSBURY
SY3 9BJ

SMDS
MADELEY COURT SCHOOL
COURT STREET, MADELEY
TELFORD TF7 5DZ
Telephone: 585704

Visiting JUNJUN AND MEIMEI IN CHINA

by Janet Whitaker

Cambridge University Press
Cambridge
New York   New Rochelle   Melbourne   Sydney

By arrangement with BBC Books, a division of BBC Enterprises Limited.

TOUCHING DOWN
IN CHINA

Junjun and Meimei live in the People's Republic of China. To visit them you'd have to fly to one of the big cities on the east coast of China. Then you'd have to take a small plane to a town called Wuhan on the banks of the Chang Jiang River. From Wuhan, you'd have to drive for an hour or take a bus to the small village of Hua Shan. Hua Shan, which means Flower Hill Village in English, is where Junjun and Meimei live.

HUA SHAN VILLAGE

So what is Junjun and Meimei's village like? Hua Shan is in flat country which is very hot in summer and very cold in winter. In spring, the fields around Hua Shan are brilliant with the yellow flowers of oil seed rape. Over half the villagers are farmers. They grow mainly rice, melons and some wheat. Because it is so hot and wet they harvest two crops of rice a year. People in Hua Shan go to work by bicycle and carry loads to and from their fields in baskets on bamboo poles on their shoulders. Only a few farmers have little tractors for hauling bigger loads. Ploughing is done by water buffaloes.

Meimei and Junjun like to visit the water buffaloes on the village threshing floor. This is where the rice is threshed after the two harvests in July and October.

In Hua Shan, the fields go right up to the houses. The village is a mixture of old houses and new ones. On some of the old houses you can see the traditional red New Year sayings pasted round the doorways to bring good luck.

JUNJUN'S FAMILY

Junjun is 10 years old and his full name is Chen Jun. (The surname always comes first in Chinese.) Junjun is his nickname and Chen is his surname. He lives with his sister Chen Ming (her nickname is Mingming) in a new house that was built by his parents Mr and Mrs Chen. Mr Chen is an untrained lawyer and Mrs Chen works in the village factory. They are very proud of their new house. They had to

save up for a long time to get enough money to be able to afford to knock down their old single storey house and put a new two-storey one in its place.

The front door leads straight into the front room. There is very little furniture, and no carpet, curtains or wallpaper, as these are all luxuries in China. But on the wall there is a beautiful and bright poster of calligraphy (Chinese writing). People in China love putting up posters to decorate their walls. There is a ceiling fan to cool the room in summer when it gets very hot.

The family keep gaily decorated vacuum flasks on the table. They always keep these flasks ready filled with hot water so that they can offer guests tea at any time. The family also use them for drinking water as water straight from the tap is not safe enough to drink and Chinese stoves in the countryside are not suitable for boiling kettles.

In the kitchen at the back, Junjun often helps his mother and his grandmother prepare the evening meal. His job is to fetch wood for the two stoves. Junjun's mother cooks rice on the little stove, while his grandmother chops up vegetables and meat ready to cook quickly in the wok on the big stove.

She cuts the food into small pieces to make it easier to eat with chopsticks. Junjun mixes soya sauce into some spinach. Often, in the evening, the Chen family eats green vegetables and rice with pork or fish, followed by soup. Junjun's mother says that country children always like to eat rice with their meals, so usually it's only the adults who have steamed buns and noodles instead of rice. But Junjun's favourite breakfast is fried doughnut sticks and buns with spring onions inside, which his father buys for the family from a nearby restaurant.

Junjun is very lucky to have a bedroom all of his own. If he lived in the city it would be impossible, because the houses are too crowded there. But in the countryside there is more room, so the Chens planned their new house with a room each for both Junjun and Mingming. Junjun has his own desk and on it his most prized possession, a radio. On his walls are a calendar with a picture of a famous film actress and some calligraphy. Some of the calligraphy is written by Junjun himself, as he wants to be a calligrapher when he grows up, like his grandfather was before him.

Junjun's other grandfather often helps the family with their vegetable plot. Junjun's grandfather used to work for the state bank but now he's retired and has a state pension. They all go to work in the garden about three evenings a week after school and work. They grow enough vegetables to feed the whole family – grandparents as well. They grow peppers, sweetcorn, tomatoes, chinese cabbage, spinach and chives. While Junjun's mother picks leaves for the evening meal, Mingming weeds, and grandfather and father hoe with long and short hoes. Junjun's job is to ladle the

manure onto the vegetables. This is called 'night soil' manure and is a mixture of specially treated human, pig and water buffalo sewage collected by the village people in carts.

Junjun's mother takes the fresh vegetables she's picked back home to get the evening meal started. Sometimes Junjun's father has to work late and often can't get back home in the evening, as he works in another village and it's too far to bicycle at night. Junjun's mother sometimes has to go back to her factory at night, as she has to take turns to help guard it, or she may go to a meeting at the factory. It's lucky that the grandparents live near by and can babysit for Junjun and Mingming.

Sometimes Junjun and Mingming are allowed to watch the television which is in their parents' bedroom, but usually they have to do their homework instead. Junjun's parents are quite strict about homework being done first.

MEIMEI'S FAMILY

Across the village the grandmother of eight-year-old Meimei helps to look after her grandchildren. Meimei's full name is Yuan Mei, her little brother Fengfeng's is Yuan Feng. The Yuan family live in a much smaller and older house than Junjun's family. Their single storey house has only two rooms and a very small kitchen. It stands in a courtyard with eight other houses.

There's a little yard at the back of the house where Meimei feeds the chickens and newly hatched chicks and where Mrs Yuan puts the washing out.

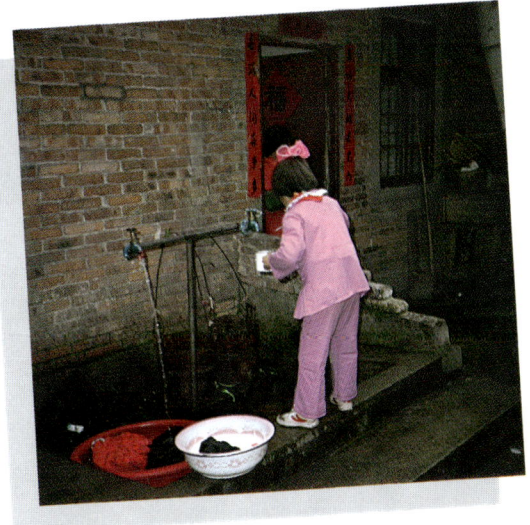

In the courtyard there are taps shared by all eight houses and it's there that Meimei cleans her teeth every morning before going to school. All the family's water comes from these taps and has to be carried into the house – like Junjun's house, there is no bathroom. Meimei's grandmother checks that Meimei washes herself properly in the big enamel bowl kept in the front room. Meimei and Fengfeng have a bath only once a week, as the water has to be heated and it takes a long time.

Although Mrs Yuan doesn't have a bathroom she does have a washing machine. She keeps it in the front room along with the television set and she's very proud of it. It's only recently that families like the Yuans and the Chens have been able to save up for things like black and white television sets and washing machines.

As there are only two rooms in the house, Mr and Mrs Yuan sleep in the front room on the sofa, which opens out into a bed, while Meimei and Fengfeng share the back bedroom. In the morning everybody gets up when the cocks are crowing, at about 6.00 a.m. While the children dress, Meimei's father makes the breakfast of rice porridge with eggs or pickled vegetables, while Meimei's mother sweeps the floor and brings in water to heat for the vacuum flasks. Meimei and Fengfeng sometimes play badminton in the courtyard before breakfast.

Meimei sometimes wears an orange tracksuit for going to school. Chinese children often wear tracksuits, and they all like to wear trainers too. Mrs Yuan enjoys dressing Meimei up for special occasions and likes her to wear her cotton trouser suits, usually in lilac or pink, with black cotton slippers. If it's cold, Meimei wears a jumper under her suit. She only wears a coat of padded cotton in the very coldest weather. Fengfeng has a military-style jacket that he likes to wear and Junjun has one of these too. Clothes for children are usually very brightly coloured compared with the navy or khaki cotton trouser suits that many adults wear.

In the evenings Meimei has to do her homework too, often with her father helping her. Sometimes she will do some painting, which is her favourite hobby. The family often play cards or chess, both of which are favourite Chinese games. Because the house is so small the TV set isn't switched on until Meimei has finished her homework. The television set has to be switched off when the children go to bed, as the sound would keep them awake.

GOING TO SCHOOL WITH JUNJUN AND MEIMEI

Junjun and Meimei go to school six days a week. The junior school is right in the centre of the village and they have to be there by 7.30 a.m. On Monday mornings first thing there is a special ceremony in the playground, the raising of the National Flag. Every school playground in China has a very tall flagpole and the red flag of the People's Republic of China, with the five yellow stars, is always to be seen fluttering at the top. As class leader, Junjun takes his turn in hoisting the flag while the national anthem plays over the speakers and his schoolmates give the salute of the Young Pioneers.

Meimei and Junjun are members of the Young Pioneers, an organisation run by the government. They always wear red scarves round their necks and their special salute is a bent arm raised above the head.

十四

A special teacher in each school organises the Young Pioneers. At school the Pioneers are expected to help the teachers, keep the classrooms tidy, write up the notices and the school magazine on the blackboards at the back of every classroom and generally be good pupils. As class leader, Junjun has to check that all his classmates are wearing their red scarves. The scarf represents a corner of the red national flag, red for the blood spilt in the Revolution of 1949 which put the Communist Party in power. After school the Young Pioneers go on trips to East Lake Park or the Children's Palace in Wuhan. Sometimes they visit places of historical interest or attend basketball and ping pong matches. The children also help old people in the village. Junjun and Meimei enjoy going to the Young Pioneers' summer camp every year.

CALLIGRAPHY

Lessons start at 8.00 a.m. Children in Meimei's class spend a lot of their time learning to read and write Chinese. It's a very difficult language. It doesn't have an alphabet. Instead, Meimei has to learn the sign, called the character, for each word. She has to know hundreds of characters in order to be able to read a story. The characters were originally based on pictures of the things they represented. Here are some of them:

Old			Modern	
Water	氺	(running water)	水	Shui (pronounced Shway)
Field	田	(divided fields)	田	Tian (pronounced Tee-en)
Moon	⽉	(crescent moon)	月	Yue (pronounced Yu-eh)
Child	子	(small person)	子	Haizi (pronounced Hi-dze)

Learning to write Chinese takes a lot of practice too. Chinese handwriting is called calligraphy and the Chinese think it is very important to do it well. Both Meimei and Junjun enjoy doing calligraphy. They use brushes and ink. They sometimes use bottled ink in school, but calligraphy should really be done with ink made from a solid ink block which is mixed with water on a special ink stone. Into the ink they dip brushes of different thicknesses and make thick strokes and thin strokes. Junjun says that you have to get the strength of the stroke right for big characters but at the same time you have to be very delicate for small ones. The spacing of the strokes and the space between the characters is important. He would never draw the character first in pencil – that's not the way to do good calligraphy! When Junjun writes, he starts in the top right-hand corner and goes down instead of across the page.

Junjun has one lesson a week which Meimei doesn't have yet and that's a morality class. The children read stories about the way people behave and about knowing the difference between right and wrong. Each week the teacher discusses a story with the pupils.

One week, Junjun was learning about friendship and had to give some examples of what good friendship meant. Another week Junjun learnt about not being envious of other people.

17 十七

DOING DRILL

Every day Junjun leads his class out on to the playground for drill. There is no gymnasium or hall at the school, so all the children in the school do their exercises together in the playground. Music plays over the loudspeaker and tells them what to do. All over China children do the same exercises to the same music. One day a visitor came to judge their drill. Junjun's class didn't do very well because they hadn't practised enough and weren't all in time with the music. They did much better in the races held at the end of the week, when Junjun cheered his team on.

There are some other gymnastics that Junjun and Meimei do every day along with all the children in China. These are eye excercises. Music and instructions are played over a loudspeaker. The children sit at their desks, roll their eyes, and rub points on their cheeks and the bridges of their noses. These exercises are intended to relax the eyes and help their eyesight. They do them twice a day between lessons.

As well as calligraphy, morality and Chinese, Junjun's other lessons are the same as those in other countries, such as geography, art, nature study and maths. Instead of using a calculator in maths, Junjun and Meimei learn how to use an abacus. This is a counting frame that is used everywhere in China, even in shops, where it is used instead of a cash till. Once you know how to use it, it is very quick and easy. It is said that a quick person can use an abacus faster than they can use a calculator.

PLAYTIME

At playtime, Meimei plays games like 'drop handkerchief' with a group of girls from her class. Sometimes they get a long skipping rope turning and the boys join in as well. The older boys prefer to play ping pong, which is a national sport in China, on large stone tables in the playground. Junjun enjoys playing football too. He doesn't know a lot about other countries outside China but he does know about the main British football teams like Liverpool and Arsenal!

OFF TO WORK

While Junjun and Meimei are at school their parents go to work. Junjun's father works in a nearby village and bicycles there every day.

He used to be a peasant working on the land. Now he is a local government official, called a cadre, and he deals with matters of law. He's paid by the village government and earns 100 yuan a month. He isn't a trained lawyer but he talks to people about their problems to see if he can help. If the problem is too complicated he passes his clients on to a proper lawyer. Most of the problems are to do with marriage quarrels or property matters. He will explain the law and then send the person to their neighbourhood committee and ask them to sort out the problem. Every area has a neighbourhood committee, mainly made up of retired people who use their wisdom to sort out local problems, keep the peace, and make sure people observe the Government campaigns. These campaigns can vary from simple ones like "No Litter" to the more important campaign to persuade couples not to have more than one child. This campaign started in about 1980 to try to stop China's population from growing any more.

1 yuan = about 23 pence/ 40 cents (US)/44 cents (Canadian)

Junjun's mother works in the village clothing factory in the centre of Hua Shan. She works at a sewing machine making shorts, jackets and shirts. Until recently, however, she worked in the fields farming the family's plot of land.

It was because she worked so hard at farming that the family saved up enough money to rebuild their house. Now she earns less in the factory but the work is a lot easier. She's paid by the factory, which is owned by the village, and earns 65 yuan a month plus a bonus of about 20 yuan if she works well.

When she worked in the fields, Junjun's mother worked under the new 'Responsibility System'. This means that she rented her land from the village and as rent she gave part of her crops back to the government. She could keep the rest of her crops for herself and sell them in the local 'free' market and keep the money. She was responsible for what she grew and how she sold it, and for what she spent the money on. This extra money helped Mr and Mrs Chen to build their new house. Under the old system Hua Shan was a commune. All the people in the area round Hua Shan worked together. Junjun and Meimei's parents used to work for the Hua Shan commune. The system was changed by the government a few years ago and the communes have mostly been abolished. The new Responsibility System was then started and now people work much more for themselves.

Junjun's mother mainly grew vegetables and fruit but some of the farmers now grow rice, oil seed rape, melons and tea. The rice farming is very hard work, as rice likes to grow in water and the wet soil has to be turned over in the spring ready for the rice seedlings.

Water buffaloes are the best animals for ploughing rice fields, because they are very strong and they like water. It's not so pleasant for the farmer who's raking the wet soil behind the buffalo! After the seedlings are put in the ground by hand, they are covered over with plastic sheets to help them grow faster. Then, when the seedlings have grown about 15cm (6 inches), they are pulled up again by hand and transplanted to other fields, where they are spread out more widely. A few months later, in July, they are harvested and then the farmer starts all over again for a second harvest in October. It's back-breaking work.

23 二十三

GOING SHOPPING IN HUA SHAN

The farmers are now the wealthy people in the village and they want to have things to spend their money on. Meimei's mother is the person to help them. She works in the big department store that is at the centre of the village. The most expensive things she sells are televisions, radios and cassette-players, which everybody wants to have. At Chinese New Year, when everyone treats themselves to something new, the department store sells right out of televisions. Most of the time Meimei's mother sells more everyday things, such as the brightly coloured vacuum flasks and the enamel bowls and mugs that everyone uses.

She adds up the cost of purchases on her abacus on the counter and then puts the money in a drawer at the back. The store sells everything people in the village need, including bicycles, but it doesn't sell food.

When Meimei's mother goes shopping every day in her lunch break, she can either go to the state-owned butcher's shop or to the 'free' market. She buys pork from a farmer who has killed one of his pigs and is selling the meat for his own profit.

Next Meimei's mother goes to buy some mushrooms and some doufu at a nearby stall. Doufu is soya-bean curd and can be bought in flat sheets, spongy squares, and many other shapes and textures. It is often eaten chopped up with vegetables in place of meat and is a very good source of protein.

The stall holder weighs mushrooms and doufu on small portable scales which he balances by hand. There are lots of other vegetables on sale in the market – cauliflowers, root ginger, Chinese cabbage with lots of stalk, spinach and the very strange white bulbous plant called lotus root, covered in mud because it grows under water. There are many herbs and spices too on sale, some for use in cooking and some for use in medicine.

Meimei likes the fruit stalls, because they sell sweet drinks and fresh coconut as well as apples and pears. Later in the year they sell plums and fresh melon. She's been told not to buy the tempting big sticks of sugar cane at the front of the stall, as they're not good for her teeth.

The market doesn't only sell food. There's a stall selling clothes and in front of it an old gentleman cuts out dress material while his elderly wife sews the pieces together. Customers choose their material and pattern and their garment is made up for them straight away – except when it rains of course. There's also a shoe repairer out on the kerb side, and sometimes a visiting hairdresser and even a dentist who sets up shop in the open air market. There's also a man selling what looks like rats' tails, but it's actually the rat poison he's selling and the tails are to prove it works!

There are other little shops in the main street, such as the post office, the hardware shop, and many grocer's shops selling rice, buns, biscuits, noodles and soya sauce. But there are no supermarkets and no frozen foods and very little food in tins and packages. Nearly all the food Junjun and Meimei eat is freshly bought and prepared at home.

KITE FESTIVAL

Every year in the spring there is a kite festival in Hua Shan village. Kite flying is very popular with both children and adults and the schools in the area all send in competitors. This year, Junjun was one of the ones chosen to represent his school.

Everybody sat on a high grassy embankment, which is a flood dyke for the Chang Jiang river. The dyke top is perfect for running along and getting a good wind behind the kite. Everyone laid their kites out on the grass while speeches were made and the judges described how they were going to judge the competition. They were going to judge how well the kite was made, whether it flew high, whether it had lots of movement in the sky, and, if there were several kites flown together, whether they moved well as a group.

The best made kite was definitely the giant dragon kite, nearly 60 feet long, which was laid out in front of the crowd. Junjun said it would never fly and, although twenty people had a go at getting it up into the air, he was right, it was just too long! Most people's kites were simpler.

Junjun had made his own kite out of thin strips of bamboo covered with tissue paper. He had then painted the tissue paper with ancient Chinese mythical people, called 'immortals'. The kite fell down when he first tried to fly it, but with some help from his friends he tried again, racing along the dyke top, with the kite getting higher and higher. Junjun didn't win the competition but he was very pleased with the way his kite had flown. There were two kites which he thought were marvellous. One looked like a rocket – and drew an Ooh! of admiration from the crowd. The other one was a beautiful group of butterflies which were made of thinnest silk so that they fluttered their painted wings as they swooped around together. Everyone agreed it had been a wonderful afternoon.

A DAY OUT IN WUHAN

Sunday is the only time when all the family can have a day off together, so the Chens and the Yuans like to do something special on that day. Going out of the village is the biggest treat of all for Meimei and Junjun. They have to go on the bus, as very few people have their own cars in China.

About an hour's drive away is the big city of Wuhan which is the furthest either Junjun or Meimei has travelled. Their parents have taken them to East Lake Park where there are boats, pagodas, cafés and statues of famous Chinese heroes such as the poet Qu Yuan. On a Sunday, the park is crowded with thousands of people, all enjoying their day off. The biggest treat of all, though, for Junjun and Meimei, is to go right into the centre of Wuhan to the shops. Here it is noisy with traffic and pop music and very, very crowded, but the shops sell all sorts of exciting things which can't be found in the little department store in Hua Shan. It's all much more lively than the village.

THE FUTURE

Both Meimei and Junjun know that there is a much bigger world outside their quiet village of Hua Shan, but it will be a few years yet before they can think of exploring it. One day they hope to visit the Great Wall of China, and maybe even go abroad. The China they are growing up in has seen great changes in the last 50 years and there will, no doubt, be even greater changes in the future. China wants to become a wealthier country but it wants a better standard of living for *all* its people and everyone will have to help each other to achieve this. Whatever Junjun and Meimei do in the future, they and their parents want it to be for the good of their country as well as for themselves.

INDEX

Abacus 19, 24

Bicycles 4, 21
Breakfast 7, 12

Cadre 21
Calligraphy (Chinese writing) 6, 8, 16, 17
Chang Jiang (Yangzi River) 3, 28
Chinese language 16
Chopsticks 7
Clothes 13
Communes 22

Dinner 7

Eye exercises 19

Factory work 9
Farming 4, 22, 23
Flower Hill Village 3
Food 7, 25, 26, 27

Games 12, 13, 15, 20

Hua Shan 3, 4, 23
Houses 6, 7, 8, 10, 11, 12

Junjun's house 6, 7, 8
Junjun's mother 6, 9, 22
Junjun's father 9, 21

Kites (or Kite Festival) 28, 29

Meimei's house 10, 11, 12
Meimei's mother 10, 11, 12, 13, 24, 25
Meimei's father 12, 13
Money 21, 22

Neighbourhood Committee 21
New Year 5, 24
Night soil manure 9

One Child Campaign 21

Physical Education
 (Drill) 18
 (eye exercises) 19

Responsibility system 22, 23
Rice 4, 23

School 14, 15, 16, 17, 18, 19, 20
Shops and markets 24, 25, 26, 27, 30

Television 9, 11, 13, 24

Vacuum flasks 7, 12, 24
Vegetables 7, 25, 26

Water buffalo 5, 9, 23
Woks 7
Wuhan 3, 15, 30

Young Pioneers 14, 15